Astrology

The ultimate guide to astrology and the 12 Zodiac signs, horoscopes, and using Astrology for success, romance, wealth, discovering your destiny, and more!

Table Of Contents

Introduction

I want to thank you and congratulate you for downloading the book, "Astrology".

This book contains helpful information about astrology, what it is, and how to use it.

You will soon learn about the history of astrology, and how this science was created and works.

You will also learn about the 12 zodiac signs, and discover how these affect you depending on the date you were born.

You will gain a greater understanding of horoscopes, and learn how they are created, and the meanings behind them.

This book will explain to you tips and techniques that will allow you to begin successfully changing your life with the help of astrology and the power of the zodiac signs!

Whether you're a complete skeptic, or you have experienced the power of astrology before, this book will have something to offer you in the way of education, and guidance for the future.

Thanks again for downloading this book, I hope you enjoy it!

Chapter 1:
Astrology: The Basics

Astrology is such a broad subject that a single book is essentially not enough to explain its different facets. However popular it may be, there are still a lot a lot of people who are not into astrology. Many people frown on it and its principles because they misunderstand it, and the science behind it.

This book aims to provide you with a proper understanding of your traits and characteristics based on your date of birth. In this book, you will learn that there is a logical explanation for every person's character traits.

Astrology

The planets, the stars, and the whole galaxy have always fascinated a lot of people. There are cultures that refer to the stars and other heavenly bodies for guidance in their everyday lives.

Astrology is the study of how the planets move and how their movements influence a person's birth. It is safe to say that astrology teaches us that your life has already been "written in the stars" and that it is just up to you to follow your "destiny".

Is it a science, then? It can be categorized as metaphysics, which refers to the study of things that are beyond what you and I feel and see. It can be likened to other fields that are founded on ancient theories of patterns and energy, such as acupuncture and yoga.

What Is the Celestial Clock?

The principles of astrology are derived from the movements of the planets that are said to influence the "Moments of Time".

Human beings are a part of the Universe. This means that your individual moments of birth are recorded on the Celestial Clock. The continuous movements of the planets and other heavenly bodies have a direct influence on your life.

Significant Names in Astrology

- Ptolemy (2nd Century AD) – He was one of the founders of astrology and astronomy. He wrote *Tetrabiblos*, the first comprehensive manual on astrology.

- Al Biruni (10th to 11th Centuries) – He is the author of the *Book of Instruction in the Elements of the Art of Astrology*, an astrological tutorial. He is also known as the source of a number of works about astronomy, physics, geography, and medicine.

- Parecelsus (15th to 16th Centuries) – He is a famous healer who considered astrology as an integral part of his art. He coined the term "pseudo-medic", referring to a doctor who knows nothing about astrology. He believed that the remedy of all illnesses can be found in the sky.

- Tycho Brahe (16th Century) – Popularly known as the "King of Astronomers". He was both an alchemist and an astrologer.

- Johannes Kepler (16th to 17th Centuries) – He was known as a great astronomer. His laws are still being used up to this day in calculating the orbits of spaceships. His first astrological almanac accurately predicted an extremely cold winter and the Turks' invasion of Austria. He was called a prophet because of this.

- Karl Gustav Jung (19th to 20th Centuries) – He was a popular psychiatrist and psychologist who studied and religiously used astrology in all his works.

Main Branches of Astrology

- *Natal Astrology* is about the human life on an individual level. This is where the birth chart (also referred to as horoscope of birth or natal chart) belongs. The reference is a map drawn in the sky during an individual's birth as seen from that person's birthplace. Natal Astrology contains *synastry,* the astrology of relationships, and astrological healing.

- *Mundane Astrology* encompasses the life of big communities of people, like cities, countries, and the world as a whole. The specific birth of a particular entity cannot be established through this branch of Astrology. Who can actually say when exactly a city or a country was "born"? Different types of astrological charts are used in this branch of Astrology. Included in this branch are political astrology, financial astrology, astrology of business, and astrometeorology.

- *Judicial Astrology* became almost non-existent at the beginning of the 20th century and it is just recently that it has been revived. This branch is considered mysterious; it is far from science but almost closer to ancient magic. The most known principles included are horary astrology, wherein a chart is cast for the time a question was asked, and elective astrology, which tells us how to select the most appropriate moment for several humane initiatives.

The Horoscopes

All of the branches of Astrology and other disciplines share one tool, the *Horoscopes*. These are schematic maps of the sky at the particular moment of time. Included are the horoscopes of birth, calculated from the time of an individual's birth and the place of birth; the horoscope of important events, and the horoscopes of equinoxes.

Experts say that this is where *"what is above"* is joined by *"what is below"*. The map is used to show the state of the universe and to be used on an individual. The term horoscope has been used for thousands of years. However, the meaning of *horoscopes* today is quite different for the word is now used to pertain to astrological and pseudo-astrological writings that Western astrologers do not actually use.

The succeeding chapters will dwell on the 12 Zodiac Signs and how they are used and interpreted.

Chapter 2:
The Twelve Signs of the Zodiac

So, we now know that Astrology involves studying the correlations of "celestial events" with the earth's behavior, specifically those that cannot be explained by magnetism, gravity, or other forces recognized by physics and other branches of science.

A "celestial event" refers to an event in the sky. The rising of the sun is considered a celestial event. Two planets being seen is a celestial event. A celestial event can involve any of the celestial bodies: the sun, the moon, any of the planets, a comet, an asteroid, a star, a quasar, and others.

Astrology has been widely used by different civilizations, but it remains to be controversial. For one, it has no scientific basis and is often viewed as bordering on superstition.

The Twelve Signs of the Zodiac

The literal meaning of the term *"zodiac"* is animals. Zodiac in Astrology means the configurations of the 12 creatures as seen in a starry night. These signs are more popularly known as the horoscope charts. They can either be masculine or feminine. The masculine signs include *Aries, Libra, Aquarius, Gemini, Sagittarius,* and *Leo.* These signs are considered to be more active and less receptive. They are more focused on the spiritual or mental world.

The feminine signs, on the other hand, are *Virgo, Cancer, Taurus, Capricorn Pisces,* and *Scorpio.* They are the opposites of the masculine signs. They are more receptive and less active and their focus is primarily on the emotional or material world.

The Quatermaries

Quatermaries mean three in number. The 12 zodiac signs can also be grouped into 3 categories, consisting of four signs each: the Cardinal Signs, Fixed Signs, and Mutable Signs.

Cardinal Signs

These include *Aries, Libra, Capricorn,* and *Cancer.* These signs are said to be signs of movement, great vitality, and dynamic change.

Fixed Signs

Included in this category are *Aquarius, Taurus, Scorpio,* and *Leo.* They are signs of stability, fixity, and earthiness. People under these signs are said to have great willpower.

Mutable Signs

These signs are *Virgo, Pisces, Sagittarius,* and *Gemini.* They are conceived to be adaptable to change. They are capable of modifying according to the conditions and circumstance they are subjected to.

The 12 Signs

According to an individual's birth date, these are the different signs of the zodiac:

1. Aries, The Ram – March 21 to April 19

2. Taurus, The Bull – April 20 to May 20

3. Gemini, The Twins – May 21 to June 20

4. Cancer, The Crab – June 21 to July 22

5. Leo, The Lion – July 23 to August 22

6. Virgo, The Maiden – August 23 to September 22

7. Libra, The Scales – September 23 to October 22

8. Scorpio, The Scorpion – October 23 to November 21

9. Sagittarius, The Centaur – November 22 to December 21

10.Capricorn, The Mountain Goat – December 22 to January 19

11. Aquarius, The Man who Carries Water – January 20 to February 18

12. Pisces, The Fish – February 19 to March 20

In the next chapters, you will learn more about these signs, their perceived general characteristics, their attributes, and all the other information about them.

Chapter 3:
The Cardinal Signs: *Aries, Libra, Capricorn,* and *Cancer*

Aries, The Ram

Aries is a fire sign that is ruled by the planet, Mars.

Symbol:

Aries is represented by an image of a ram.

General Characteristics:

Individuals under this sign are courageous, willful, energetic, leading, and commanding. They often emerge as leaders even when they have to become a follower.

An Aries is considered to be full of life. The typical Aries individual is highly energetic. The people under this sign are constantly looking for challenges.

An Aries person is full of vitality. They are always curious. They are always on a quest for justice.

They excel in almost anything they venture into. They enjoy having competition in their every endeavor because it becomes their motivating factor to succeed. Challenges are what drive them. If they are given the opportunity to win over someone and showcase their skills and abilities, Aries is always "in it to win it".

People under the sign of Aries are most alive when they are able to control other people; hence, they are good candidates to become leaders. They are mostly impatient; particularly with people they consider not to be their equals. They dislike being instructed on what to do if they know that the one in charge is inferior to them.

Being a fire sign, an Aries person is bright, warm, and vital. They usually have hot temperaments and are highly impulsive. When they have wronged someone, they do not hesitate to make amends.

Aries is highly optimistic and does not resort to nurturing negative thoughts, thus, they do not tolerate the ones who do.

Good: Because of their energetic nature, it is not difficult for them to work for long hours. They often initiate breakthroughs. They are thorough and have a knack for keeping accurate records. They are passionate about life and love.

Bad: They can become selfish because of their passion to achieve anything they put their mind into. They can have a low tolerance to people who are not their equals. Most people under the sign of Aries often feel unappreciated for what they have accomplished so they resort to sarcasm and rudeness.

Libra, The Scales

Libra is an air sign, whose ruling planet is Venus.

Symbol:

It is symbolized by a pair of scales.

General Characteristics:

They generally have a good sense of justice and are endlessly seeking for beauty. They are in constant search for a sense of balance between leisure and career, as well as an equal balance in their emotional and physical (or spiritual) lives. As a result of this trait, they tend to become tentative when making decisions, because they weigh all possible scenarios and options. The good thing is that they end up making the best decision all the time.

They are happiest when everyone they love is living in peace and harmony, hence, their endless quest for balance.

Good: Libra people have a good sense of fair play and they become disappointed if there is something unfair going on. They have a knack for talking non-stop, especially if they are talking about their favorite conversation topics. Generally, they make decisions based on the good of most people. They do not hesitate to resort to sacrificing their own happiness or satisfaction just for the benefit of their family or group.

Bad: Since they take too long when it comes to decision-making, they can be viewed as lazy and absent minded. Also, because of their desire to get justice all the time, they tend to be argumentative to the point of being inappropriate. They do not necessarily want to be in charge but they want to have their voices heard.

Capricorn, The Mountain Goat

Capricorn is an earth sign and its ruling planet is Saturn.

Symbol:

It is represented by a mountain goat.

General Characteristics:

Capricorns are goal oriented, driven, and extremely ambitious people. They are willing to do anything just to realize their goals. Their self-discipline works for them because it helps them to succeed. Some of the world's most recognized leaders, teachers, and scientists are under the sign of Capricorn.

They take life seriously because achievement and success are everything to them. They are known to be natural-born leaders, diplomats, politicians, and mathematicians. Because they are dead set on achieving their goals, they have the tendency to guard their hearts closely. It is not easy to get close to a Capricorn person but if you do get through them, it will be worth it.

Good: Capricorns are known to make realistic and logical decisions. They are family-oriented; however, they stay guarded when they perceive that their family could bring them harm. They can be quite sarcastic and have a terrible sense of humor, but most often than not, their witty sarcasm helps in finding humor in just about anything. They are highly analytic and intellectual.

Bad: Because they are determined and dedicated to achieving their goals, they come off as dull to other people who do not understand their internal nature. They may look emotionless on the outside, but their minds are always in overdrive. They come off as selfish because of their desire to succeed on their own. They can go to the extreme of strategically withholding important information for their own benefit. They have the tendency to refuse to face reality for fear that may have made a mistake or have done something that they didn't like.

Cancer, The Crab

Cancer is a water sign that is ruled by the Moon.

Symbol:

The symbol of Cancer is a crab.

General Characteristics:

They are generally emotional; often seeking security from other people. They are family/group oriented.

The sign's image representation is very apt with their characteristics. Just as a crab brings its own shell on its back, so does a typical Cancer person. Family and the home are everything to them; they remain dedicated in spite of challenges.

Crabs generally move sideways as opposed to straight forward movements, a typical Cancerian is also like that. For instance, a Cancer person avoids a fight and would move to another direction to avoid arguments. If there is an alternative way, they will find it just to avoid confrontations and/or challenges, even if it would take them longer to reach their destination.

They have difficulty letting go of someone or something that makes them happy. The main point to a Cancerian's existence is to be needed. They often need validation that they matter to someone they care about. They want to be reassured; because that is the only way they will feel secure in the relationship.

They are generally brave and protective of their loved ones. They can be timid and shy. They are loyal to their partners and their friends, but they can be moody and brooding.

Cancer is a water sign, meaning those under the sign of Cancer have a mysterious side to them.

Good: They have a good sense of humor and often find something to laugh about, even in the most mundane situations. Cancers are good listeners. A lot of people gravitate towards them because of a Cancer's nurturing and understanding nature. When a Cancer person becomes your friend, you have gained a friend for life. They are reliable and dependable. You can always count on them for help.

Bad: The bad thing about Cancers is that they are extremely moody. Their moods change from good to bad in just a matter of minutes. They tend to be clingy and unreasonably insecure, especially if they sense that they are losing a friendship or a romantic relationship. They will lie if they have to; they even fail to realize that their honesty stems from their insecurity of being alone.

Chapter 4:
The Fixed Signs: Aquarius, Taurus, Leo, and Scorpio

Aquarius, The Man who Carries Water

Aquarius is an air sign that is ruled by Uranus.

Symbol:

Its symbol is a man carrying a pitcher of water.

General Characteristics:

As its symbol implies, Aquarians are more generous with their own time and resources compared to the other signs. Because of this overwhelming generosity, they are more likely to take on humanitarian acts. They have a deeper understanding of the needs of other people and they have a great concern for the welfare of other people.

Because of these positive qualities, they are well-loved by all the people around them. They always want to be connected with others. They always want to be of assistance to others.

They have a fascination for many things, and they have a knack for inventing things. They are often perceived to have no emotions because of their flair for exchanging ideas. They are patient and have a high tolerance for other people's shortcomings.

Good: Aquarians are considered the friendliest. They are intelligent, talented, and energetic. They have excellent people skills, but they still enjoy having some time for themselves, without being disconnected from others.

Bad: When they don't get time off for themselves, they tend to succumb to depression and become devoid of emotions. They can be resentful if they are not heard. Their tendency towards self-reflection often makes them look a little eccentric.

Taurus, The Bull

Taurus is an earth sign, governed by the planet Venus.

Symbol:

The sign Taurus is symbolized by the bull.

General Characteristics:

Taurus people are generally pleasure-seekers, controlling, dependable, grounded, and sensual in nature. They can be peaceful and methodical. Their actions are always deliberate.

They enjoy all luxuries, foods, drinks, and sex. They work hard to get the luxuries they love.

They are known to be slow to anger but can become volatile once provoked and disturbed. Most often, it takes them a long time to simply decide on what they want to do with their lives.

They are more drawn to living on the countryside.

While they enjoy sex, it takes a long time for them to commit to any relationship, but once they are committed, it will be for the long run.

Good: People under Taurus always finish what they have started. They are adaptable. They can easily adjust to new challenges given them, especially if the reward can give them comfort, luxury, and sex. They have a good sense of humor.

Bad: They are perceived to be stubborn. They can be "bullies" when it comes to the ideals and principles they believe in. They always want to become leaders and they have high regard for themselves. If they are not made to lead, they resist and fail to cooperate; often going to the extent of sabotaging projects or undermining authority.

Leo, The Lion

Leo is a fire sign that is ruled by the Sun.

Symbol:

This sign has a lion as a symbol.

General Characteristics:

They are highly organized, generous, and protective. Like the lion, they are proud, always regal, and in charge. They like comfort and relaxation.

They always look at the bigger picture. They have little patience on both extremely boring and too complicated things. They are natural-born leaders and have trouble taking orders from other people.

To love and be loved is what drives Leos. They have this need to be adored and appreciated. If other people fail to recognize their contribution to a project or a solution to a problem, they feel slighted and hurt. The bottom line is they want to be noticed, heard, and appreciated.

Being a fire sign, Leos are warm and bright, characteristics that draw other people to them.

Good: They are honest and decent. They will always do what is right and won't think of any possible consequences. They are known to love luxury and material things. They are generally accepting of all kinds of people.

Bad: Because of their excessive self-worth, they are often seen as arrogant. They lean towards extravagance. They always want to be in charge.

Scorpio, The Scorpion

Scorpio is a water sign; its ruling planet is Pluto.

Symbol:

Its symbol is a scorpion.

General Characteristics:

They are passionate, reflective, exacting, and combating. They are not necessarily aggressive, but when they are provoked, they tend to fight back.

They are always waiting for their time alone. They are generally contemplative and often long to have some alone time and become totally irritated when they are not given the opportunity.

They are excellent secret-keepers. Other people are drawn to them because Scorpios have the ability to bring out the best and worst in them.

Scorpios do not fear anything. They are great risk takers. They always want to know what makes other people tick.

Good: Since they exhibit strong self-control, they also expect that from others. They are well-disciplined. They are protective of every aspect of their lives. They are always eager to get to know other people. They are generous givers and do not expect to be paid.

Bad: Scorpios never forget if you did something wrong or you hurt them. They are perceived to have invented the word "vendetta". The females are less forgiving than the males. They can also be pessimists. They also tend to have unfounded paranoia and can become overly suspicious of others.

Chapter 5:
The Mutable Signs: Virgo, Pisces, Sagittarius, and Gemini

Virgo, The Maiden

Virgo is an earth sign under the planet Mercury.

Symbol:

It is represented by a Maiden.

General Characteristics:

Like the Maiden, a Virgo person is always cool, calm, and has a good sense of clarity. They show a mild-mannered attitude, but underneath that façade, they have a flurry of activities going on. There are always a lot of things in their minds: constantly thinking, analyzing, and calculating.

They are good at creating something good out of nothing. Being left alone is not an issue for them, as long as they know that despite being alone, they are still appreciated and needed by the people they love and care about. They are excellent listeners and are good at helping others out.

Virgo people are detail-oriented, making it easier for them to create something useful and beautiful out of nothing. They are not the leader types but are smart strategists; they are the ones who you would want to have on your own team.

Good: They have a good heart for everyone. They are kind, gentle, and patient. They are excellent creative thinkers.

Bad: They have the tendency to be over zealous in having good overall health, which can lead them to become too obsessive in weight loss regimens and eating healthy. They are perceived to be the most judgmental of all the signs.

Pisces, The Fish

The sign, Pieces, is a water sign under the ruling planet Neptune.

Symbol:

A fish represents Pisces.

General Characteristics:

They are generally daydreamers. They always dream of making excellent ideas a reality, but they usually fail when it comes to taking the right actions.

They are always happy and vibrant. They care deeply for the people they love. They are extremely dedicated. They can stay in a relationship for years or can work in the same company for decades before moving on.

Some people find it hard to get to know a Piscean because they don't easily open up to other people.

Good: They are highly emphatic people and always feel the need to reach out and help people. They are kind and caring individuals.

Bad: Because they feel everything so deeply, they can become worry freaks. They worry about anything which often leads them to becoming indecisive. They don't like hurting other people's feelings to the point of lying just so they won't offend them.

Sagittarius, The Centaur

Sagittarius is a fire sign, under the planet, Jupiter.

Symbol:

It is symbolized by a centaur with a bow aiming to shoot.

General Characteristics:

People under this sign love to travel, meet new people, and learn and discover new things. They always crave for freedom, both physically and figuratively. They become unhappy and restless when they try to follow a normal routine. They want action and variety.

Good: They are intelligent and they always want to be around equally intelligent people. They are highly creative and are good at creating new things. They are very spiritual. They travel a lot to gain more knowledge and growth.

Bad: When a Sagittarian is not given enough room to grow, they tend to become resentful. They are the ones that make big and unrealistic plans, but they often fail because of a lack of follow-through.

Gemini, The Twins

Gemini is an air sign. It is governed by Mercury.

Symbol:

A pair of twins symbolizes Gemini.

General Characteristics:

From its symbol, one of the most glaring characteristics of Gemini people is revealed: they rarely do anything alone. They are at their happiest when they can share ideas with another person. Communication is a huge concern for people under this sign. They are always curious and have excellent people skills. Take them to parties and they will be the life of the party, always having something to talk about with anyone.

They are adventurous and love to travel for as long as they can. They enjoy meeting new people and experiencing new cultures and ideas.

Being an air sign, they have a certain effervescence about them that draw a lot of people to them. They never stop at achieving intellectual stimulation and they always push themselves to their limits: physically, spiritually, and mentally. They are attracted to bright colors.

Gemini people are highly intuitive; hence, they make great speakers, entrepreneurs, writers, and anything that can showcase their artistic side.

Good: They are excellent conversationalists. They are optimistic and have a good sense of humor. They don't allow boredom to creep in; they just create their own "fun moments".

Bad: They have the tendency to want to have all the attention on them. When they think that something is not going right for them, they immediately "abandon ship"; this can be their friendships, relationships, or career. They always have the desire to be seen as important, and because of this, they will twist the truth if they need to.

Chapter 6:
Using Astrology to Shape Your Own Life

The Natal Chart is an important tool when you want to use Astrology to change your life. It is based on the date, time, and place of your birth. Astrology will help you understand yourself and other people, and may guide you in finding the answers about life.

5 Tips to Help You Shape Your Own Life

1. Know the 12 Signs of the Zodiac.

    It has been detailed in the previous chapters the characteristics that differentiate each of the 12 signs from one another.

Know Yourself and Others

One important step is to understand yourself and others. Understanding the inner qualities of your "Sun sign" leads you to a better insight of the personality of others and yourself. This will help you to learn why people act the way they do. The Sun is the focal point and the planets move around it.

The Elements

You might have noticed the mention of the elements in the previous chapters.

- *Earth* – This is the element of stability. *Taurus, Virgo,* and *Capricorn* are Earth signs. They dislike unpredictability and always want to see tangible results.

- *Air* – This is the element of thought and communication. *Gemini, Libra,* and *Aquarius* are Air signs. They are thinkers and intellectual analyzers.

- *Water* – This is the element of emotion. *Cancer, Scorpio,* and *Pisces* are Water elements. They can be enmeshed in emotional roller coaster.

- *Fire* – The element of fire is associated with Aries, Leo, and Sagittarius. Those graced by the fire element are often enthusiastic, and larger than life.

2. Learn your Astrological Chart.

While the Sun is an integral part of the astrological interpretation, there are still other celestial bodies that provide additional insights. For instance, the Moon sign gives information about human emotions. It would help to consult an experienced astrologer. Prepare your own set of questions and get into it with an open mind. Your power of intention will help you to have a clearer and more open consultation. You can expect that the right knowledge will be presented to you at a perfect time and your astrologer would be the best "medium".

It will be easier to evaluate what your astrologer can contribute. A good astrologer will not dwell on negativity but focus more on the positive.

3. Go to an astrologer at least once a year.

The best time to see your astrologer is just before your birthday. There is a great significance when you get a reading close to your birthday. The astrologer has a variety of tools, one of which is the Solar Return. Every year, when the Sun returns to its same exact place where it was "born", the astrologer may cast a chart that will reveal what is in store for you in the coming year.

4. Plan and act based on the Lunar Cycles.

    Recognizing the flow of nature is a good practice, but with the way lives are lived today, it may be hard to pay attention to the normal cycles of nature. However, it is important to be aware of the power that actually lies deep in your own being, the place where the *Law of Attraction* works best.

    The New Moon signals growth and new beginnings. The Full Moon signals a time for harvest. An experienced astrologer would be able to assist you on what to do.

5. Trust.

    This may be the most difficult thing to do. It is easy to study astrology and how the Sun, the Moon, and other heavenly bodies affect your way of life. It is easier to believe what the Signs of the Zodiac are telling you. However, it is never easy to trust.

    Astrologers say that the ultimate lesson in astrology is that it helps you achieve the purity of heart and spirit. When you begin to focus on the positive, you change your thoughts and eventually your thoughts will influence the way you act. Astrology can help you in a number of ways. It is a powerful and amazing tool that you can use in order to manifest only the best in your life: in your relationships, career, and hopes and dreams.

    It is all about spiritually. The spirit has a great way of opening up the doors to synchronicity, just at the right moment and time, the right door will also be opened to you.

Use Astrology as a Guide

Most people who do not believe in astrology and the horoscopes think negatively of them, to the point of saying that their principles are from the devil. It may not be traditional and your religion might not approve of it, but you can still use astrology and its principles as guide to get the life that you want.

There are people who completely rely on its readings that fail to act for their own good. The problem occurs when you let astrology control your thoughts, actions, and your life in general. You still carve your own destiny, work on your own relationships, and fashion out your career, no amount of astrological readings can change your life for you.

The best thing to do is not to be too consumed and just live your life the way you want with the guidance of these astrological readings; and watch your life change for the better.

Conclusion

Thank you again for downloading this book!

I hope this book was able to help you learn more about astrology!

The next step is to put this information to use, and begin using the power of astrology to enhance your life!

Finally, if you enjoyed this book, please take the time to share your thoughts and post a review on Amazon. It'd be greatly appreciated!

Thank you and good luck!